The *E*arth
*B*ehind *M*y *T*humb

The Earth Behind My Thumb

Poems
Barbara Berkenfield

Drawings
Susan Berkenfield

SANTA FE

Poems and drawings of Section VI inspired by
the photographs of Jack Parsons in *Ordinary Beauty*.

© 2008 by Barbara Berkenfield. All Rights Reserved.

No part of this book may be reproduced in any form or by any electronic or mechanical means including information storage and retrieval systems without permission in writing from the publisher, except by a reviewer who may quote brief passages in a review.

Sunstone books may be purchased for educational, business, or sales promotional use. For information please write: Special Markets Department, Sunstone Press, P.O. Box 2321, Santa Fe, New Mexico 87504-2321.

Book and Cover design ❖ Vicki Ahl
Body typeface ❖ ITC Clearface
Printed on acid free paper

Library of Congress Cataloging-in-Publication Data
Berkenfield, Barbara, 1935-
 The earth behind my thumb : poems / by Barbara Berkenfield.
  p. cm.
 ISBN 978-0-86534-698-7 (softcover : alk. paper)
 I. Title.
PS3602.E7566E37 2008
811'.6--dc22

                                      2008034704

WWW.SUNSTONEPRESS.COM
SUNSTONE PRESS / POST OFFICE BOX 2321 / SANTA FE, NM 87504-2321 /USA
(505) 988-4418 / ORDERS ONLY (800) 243-5644 / FAX (505) 988-1025

To John,

*with thanks
for 50 special years*

CONTENTS

PREFACE / 11

I. HEROES / 13

    Rick's Globe / 17
    Arrivederci Luciano / 18
    The Earth Behind My Thumb / 20
    The Beekeeper / 23

II. SEASONS / 25

    Heaven on Earth / 29
    Back Home to Autumn / 30
    Nothing but Blue Skies / 32
    Red Moon / 34
    Summer Hummers / 35
    Winter Warning / 36
    Winter at Last / 39

III. WORLDS REAL AND IMAGINED / 41

    Stardust / 45
    A Chinese Plague / 46
    Day and Night (Navajo Legend) / 48
    Four Corners' Drive / 50
    Restore / 53
    The Innocents / 54
    Valley of the Gods / 57

IV. FAMILY AND FRIENDS / 59

    Blair's Challenge / 63
    Chautauqua Revisited / 64
    Golden Anniversary / 71
    First Born / 72
    Idaho Christmas / 74
    Heading Home / 78
    Jim's Poem / 79
    Still Dusting / 80
    The Trio / 81

V. DOG DAYS / 83

    Rill / 87
    Coco / 88
    Max / 89
    Molly / 90
    Beau / 93

VI. POEMS FOR JACK PARSONS' PHOTOGRAPHS / 95

VII. CODA / 105

    Coda II / 109

PREFACE

A Few Last Words

When my book of poetry *Driving Toward the Moon* was published in 2005, I had no thought of publishing a second volume. With that book, I had realized my goal of selecting the best of 25 years of poetry writing. As my 70th birthday was approaching, I joked that I would not have another 25 years for a second book.

I felt I had run out of time and inspiration for another project, and thought I was content with what I had accomplished. But on my milestone birthday I wrote "Today I became the age/I look but do not feel./It does fit my white hair, spots and wrinkles/But in my head/I am not yet there./Aches and pains remind me/I am no longer twenty-three./Seventy I cannot be./Not me." In light of that revelation, my "New Poems" folder has steadily expanded these past three years.

I wrote in my Preface to *Driving Toward the Moon* that "if a subject I have been mulling over wakens me in the night, I have learned to get up and write down the words in the dark. If I succumb to sleep instead, they are lost forever." I may pull off the road, stop in front of the bananas, or set down a spatula and find my small note pad to write down new ideas quickly. Even after numerous follow-up re-writes, I realize it is those first words which are the best, so I must no lose them.

Inspiration still comes at unexpected times and I am often surprised by its arrival as happened on a drive to Bluff, Utah without pen and pad at hand. The poem "Four Corners Drive" was rescued by our timely arrival at a motel where I scribbled hastily on a tiny telephone pad before the words had faded.

The poems of my first book were arranged by date within the theme sections because of the long stretch of life they covered. Poems in this book are presented alphabetically within the theme sections since they have been written within a brief span of recent aging.

Once again my theme topics have been beautifully interpreted in the drawings of my daughter-in-law Susan Berkenfield.

-Barbara Berkenfield
Santa Fe, 2008

HEROES

Rick's Globe

My hands are warmed
From holding the clay
Fired by Pueblo potters.

The lessons learned
Enable me to coil, shape and fire
My own globe.

But to make it truly mine
I break it.
Then reconstruct the shards
Into a new vessel
Repainted, refired, reborn.

March 2006:
Arthur Sze poetry workshop assignment
Subject: Rick Dillingham's pot can be seen in
the collection of the New Mexico Museum of Art.

Arrivederci Luciano

We shared a birth year.
You are gone,
While I remain,
With the sound, strength
Joy and tears
Of your voice
Resonating in my heart.

Ciao Luciano
Your talent was a gift
To all our lives.
Musician, opera lover,
Shower singer,
And those who heard
No opera aria
Before the three tenors.

Addio Pavarotti
Your joy of life
Enriched your voice.
We all loved you
For its thunder.
Larger than life,
No one can replace you.

Arrivederci Luciano
We each say good-bye
With our own fond memories
Of your grand style
And love of song.
We thank you.
Sogni d'oro.

Buenanotte Pavarotti.
Your gift of music
Came to the ears
Of all continents.
We are blessed that
Your voice will be
With us forever.
Molte grazie.

Luciano Pavarotti: "My voice is my possessor.
I am servant to my voice."
September, 2007

Earth Behind My Thumb

I remember as a child
Holding out my arm
So the moon rising over the horizon,
Huge and silver bright,
Would disappear
Behind my thumb.

Forty years ago
Jim Lovell
Did the same
From lunar orbit.
Like a child
He put his thumb over Earth
And he was stunned.

"How insignificant we are
If everything I'd ever known
Is behind my thumb."
Above a moon of darkness
Earth rose in swirling colors.
"Blues of the seas
Whites of the clouds
Salmon pink and brown of the land."

Our celebrated space travelers
Now age into their eighties.
Some already gone.
Like all memories of
My parents will vanish
When I leave,
With them go these memories
Of our planet from the moon.

Who will ride
Into moon's orbit
In the years to come
And put his thumb
Over our world?

November 2007,
Inspired by an excerpt from Tom Brokaw's *BOOM!
Voices of the Sixties* printed in the November 19
issue of *Newsweek*.

The Beekeeper

January has ever been
The month of dying.
In this yearly time of chill
I have said farewell
To parents, friends and heroes.
A call from around the world
Tells me that Ed has left us.

He once said he mostly felt
Relief in attaining
The unattainable,
And surprise that
"It happened to me
Old Ed Hillary, the beekeeper."

A sudden change
In evening's light
Makes me look up
To a grand winter view
Of our snow-dressed
Mountain peaks
Reflecting the sunset's
Blood red glow.

It is a fitting tribute,
And I raise my glass
To Ed, an "ordinary man"
The first to conquer Everest,
The top of the world,
In wonder and humility
With Tensing by his side.

Death of Sir Edmund Hillary
January 10, 2008
Conquered Mount Everest on May 29, 1953.

SEASONS

Heaven on Earth

Driving eastward
Through a pass between
Rock piled mountains
I think of drought
And the many shades of brown
In our arid world.
Then of childhood friends
Now dropping out of life,
When shaken by winter's winds,
Like the curling dry leaves
Of the mountain oaks.

Descending into Yuma
It is spring at sea level.
Near Tucson yellow flowers
Border the arrow-straight highway.
Siguaros raise their arms in salute
Against a hazy dull blue sky.
Jagged mountains zig-zag
Across the horizon
As we head home.

Evita mourns on the radio
Beau sleeps in back,
While we move forward
Through this desert diorama,
Each with thoughts unspoken.
But I wish that
We could continue driving
Together for eternity.
That would be heaven on earth.

February, 2006
Driving from California eastward on Interstate 8.

Back Home to Autumn

A great surprise greets us.
Our world is full of yellow flowers edged in blues
The fruit of a special summer
Of history-making rain.

Home again,
We hike the dog trail
Where Beau's feathered tail
Soon disappears
Like a sail
Into a sea of high grasses.

Their seeded heads
Shimmer silver and red
In the early morning light,
Swaying gently in the wind
Like wave crests across the land.

We talk of friends, family,
Twin babies on the way,
Our next trip to Mexico,
While our shoes retrace
The tracks already made
In the trail's soft sand.

Last night I read a Bible quote
"As for man, his days are as grass,
As a flower of the fields
So he flourisheth.
For the wind passeth
Over it, and it is gone;
And the place thereof
Shall know it no more."

I felt a great sadness
To be known no more.
Yet, like the seeds of these
Flowers and grasses
Finding shelter in the sandy soil,
Perhaps our children's children
Will carry us through memory
Back to life.

Santa Fe, September 2006

Nothing but Blue Skies...

July:

It is monsoon season in India,
A time of catastrophic tragedy.
Yesterday a yard of rain fell
And thousands drowned.

Yesterday in Santa Fe
July ended in record heat.
The sky returned to summer blue.
The heated haze,
Filtering mountain views,
Had disappeared.
Yet still no giant anvil clouds
Climb past the horizon.

We wait impatiently,
Scan the horizon hourly
For the annual gathering of
The thunderheads which
Herald summer storms.

A random hailstorm shreds our gardens
But soon we are parched again.
A far rumble of thunder
Sends me to my window
To watch a large black cloud
Rise above our mountains.
Then it thins and moves south,
Leaving not a drop behind.

The green grasses and wildflowers
Of spring have turned brown and sere.
Where are the summer storms,
Which bring relief

And precious inches of annual rain?
The weather map paints the Southwest hot red,
With promising storm symbols
But we are still waiting.

August:

The storm clouds arrived
Darkening our skies
But only bringing spurts
Of dusty drops.

The rains are weak
And scattered.
Cooler nights are
Our only relief.

Summer is ending
And once again
Our world is crowned
In skies of brilliant blue.

Can we be living in the same world
These last days of August
Where Hurricane Katrina
Has destroyed an entire city?

Along the Gulf coast
Devastating wind and rain
Have brought death and pain
To those who had no desire
To make history.

And thousands drowned.

Summer of 2005

Red Moon

A red moon
Hangs above the lake,
Spilling blood light
Across the water
Shivering in the
Cool night breeze.

This Harvest Moon,
Clad in the colors of war,
Recalls the heat
Of distant California fires
Sending smoke our way.

We stare
And tremble slightly,
Wrapped in the gentle mist
Of evening's mantle.

October 23, 2007
Lake Powell, Page, Arizona

Summer Hummers

Faster than the speed of light
They leave the junipers
And kamakazi dive
To possess the feeder.
As a pile-up of gray clouds
Sails sedately southward
Against the pink tinge of dawn.

Darting
Diving
Drinking
A bee-like buzzing
Wakens us.
Tiny silhouettes
Flicker into sight
Before our mountain view.

Each July
These mini dive bombers
Return to portal feeder
Fighting
Flying
Fussing
For a few weeks
Before moving on
To warmer clime.

Autumn comes
And they are gone.

Santa Fe, 2007

Winter Warning

Our mountains look old and gray,
Wrinkled like elephant skin.
No snow even at the top
To reflect the sunset glow
Even the air has no moisture
To make morning frost.

Day after winter day
Bright yellow suns march unblemished
Across the top of the weather page,
No clouds or snow
For the week ahead.
Our world is drying up.

Each day's sky is a brittle blue
As far as the hazy horizon.
The trees look rusty
The earth is dusty.
The birds are thirsty,
Searching in vain
For snow-melt puddles.

The rest of the country
Is drowning in water.
Rain and snow to north, west and east
Yet here in the Santa Fe
We are scanning the skies
For some relief.

Wildfires are raging to the south.
And we are afraid
To think of the coming spring
And the drought it brings,
As our high desert world continues
Proof of global warming.

Am I the only one
Who gets the message?

Winter, 2005-2006
Santa Fe

Winter at Last

On a mid-March Sunday
Beau and I walk out
To a world of falling snow.

He hesitates at the gate.
He has forgotten snow
During this season's
Dry winter months.

Suddenly
He bounds away
To roll, burrow, luxuriate
In the texture of snow,
While I enjoy the forgotten
Sound of silence.

No traffic noise or neighbor's voice,
No dog bark or sighing winds
Intrude on the white world around me.
I too had forgotten snow.

Spring held off today
To give us one, perhaps
Only taste of winter,
To refresh our memory
Of what has gone before.

But it is too late
To slake our coming drought,
To ease our struggle to recycle
Water from shower and sink,
Or end our fear of fire.

Santa Fe, New Mexico
March, 2006

WORLDS REAL AND IMAGINED

Stardust

He says we are made of stardust
I think he may be right.

Fallout from ancient
Exploding stars
Lands on new stars,
Enriching our earth
With life-giving molecules
Which merge for our creation.

Then is it so hard to believe
That somewhere
In this universe of stars
There is another world where
Life forms emerge from stardust?

"With chemical elements forged over 14 billion years in the fires of high-mass stares that exploded into space, and with these elements enriching subsequent generations of stars with basic ingredients of life, we are not just figuratively, but literally made of stardust."

Neil de Grasse Tyson, astrophysicist.
December 2007

A Chinese Plague

No one will stop and listen,
Look at the photos,
Read the articles
On the world of soot, smoke. and ash
Across the sea.

Taiyuan in Shanxi Province
So far away,
Three million people
Walk in the daily dark
Of coal clouds
From electric plants
Spawned by a nation's
Industrial revolution.

Cars are streaked with soot
And people gasp for breath
In a landscape
Of eternal night.

Walking up the hill
In her village gloom,
A woman fades away into
A world's devastation
More powerful than
A nuclear disaster.

Each day
A sky of coal-fired dust
From open mines
Heads our way
With hazy winds
Bringing the gift of mercury
To Oregon's bass.

Acid rain
Falls on Korea and Japan
From heavy skies,
As ozone holes expand
Above us
And our world begins to melt.

Winter, 2007
Associated Press articles and photos

Day and Night

In an early time
Night creatures wished
A world of darkness,
And day creatures wished
It always to be light.

They came to a large hogan
To play the shoe game
And decide how the world would be.
Dividing the floor in half
The teams of day and night
Gathered at opposite ends,
Each burying four moccasins
In the sandy dirt.

Behind a blanket screen
The leader of one team
Hid a ball in one moccasin.
The leader of the other team
Then guessed which shoes
Did not contain the ball.

Through the night
Back and forth,
The game continued
But neither team
Had the points to win.

Then owl became leader
And the night team
Went ahead and began
To celebrate coming victory.

Day team was suspicious
And sent gopher
To dig beneath
Night team's moccasins.

No moccasin held the ball.
Day's leader hit owl hard
And the ball fell
From 'neath his wing.
Night creatures' celebration ended
In silence.

When dawn arrived
The night animals ran home.
In his haste,
Bear put his shoes on backward
And was clubfooted ever after.

Without a winning team
The world continued as before
And we still have
Both day and night.

Navajo legend as told to me by
Steve Simpson of Twin Rocks Trading Post
March, 2006

Four Corners Drive

Cortez is left behind.
The Sleeping Ute
Stretches out beside us.
Our journey nears its end
As I head south.

The stately silhouette
Of Shiprock,
Keeper of Navajo legends,
Sails majestically into view
And I turn west.

We bisect the desolate tip of
Southeast Utah
Where harsh land
Is scrubbed bare
By ever blowing winds
Which rock our van,
Creating creaks and moans
Of protest.

Low lying cloud puffs
Stretch in strings like pearls
Across a perfect sky,
Casting shadows over
A treeless, stony land.

Shards of beer glass
Glitter like diamonds,
Reflecting sunlight
Along the roadside,
The relics of man's passing.

The road begins to bend
And sidles into curves
Descending to dry washes
And climbing shallow
Steps of table land.

No sign of life,
Patch of grass,
Glint of pond
Telephone pole
Or satellite dish
In sight.

Until we approach
Areth, slight town
Sitting among
The gas fields
Where the drilling rigs
Peck like chickens,
Up and down
Into the earth.

Climbing past
Montezuma Creek
We continue westward
Toward the San Juan River,
Enter a riparian world
Of fertile fields, tall grasses
Sandy banks.
And the glint
Of water shivering
In the breeze.

The wide valley
Between high mesas
Is clad in the autumn golds
Of cottonwood and willow
As we follow

The red cliffs
To the tiny town of Bluff
Where we are
Always welcomed back
Into a family embrace.

This womb of beauty
Is a timeless place
Of Navajo traditions
Woven into rug and basket
Or carved in cottonwood.

The vitality of designs
Dazzle us
In a trading post
Nestled against a cliff
Protected by
The Navajo Twins
Who, fixed in stone,
Tower above us.

Drive from Cortez, Colorado to Bluff, Utah
October 2007

Restore

Today I deleted a file
In My Pictures,
Accidently.
In the Recycle Bin
I clicked on
"Restore this item"
And instantly
It was back in place.

Last week a wife and mother
Woke refreshed
And drove off for her day,
Unaware it was her last.
An inexperienced driver
Turning his head to find a friend,
Drifted across the line
And she was gone.

What if those left behind,
With only the memory of her
Forever in their lives,
Could click on
"Restore this item"
And get her back?

And if all those who have died
In this weary war
Could be found in the Recycle Bin
I would click on "Restore These Items"
To bring them them back again.

July, 2007

The Innocents

Trees in flower
New blades of grass
Everywhere a delicate
Haze of green
Announces spring.

Its soft beauty
Never to be seen again
Its fragrant smells
Never to be sensed again
By more than thirty innocents.

A young man
Whose anger, hate, and pain
Baked within his brain
Became a time-bomb
Exploding in gun fire,
A human weapon
Of mass destruction.

Who knew that April morning
Their lives would end without warning
When they went into a classroom
Not a battlefield?

As my years diminish
I think I have heard the worst
And can no longer mourn.
But this cannot be ignored
And will make me weep
Until a poem is born.

Student and teacher,
Each holds a special story
Of love, dreams, and sacrifice,
Goals within reach
Accomplishments achieved.

Each one is uniquely grieved
By friends and families
With lives bereft
And ever changed.

Those random bullets,
Like pebbles tossed on water,
Have caused ripples
Throughout the world,
Reaching all of us.

We share the pain
Of a father in Puerto Rico
Holding a portrait of his son
In cap and gown.
Embraced by his brother
His grief is beyond bearing.

April, 2007
Virginia Tech

Valley of the Gods

I stare ahead
Until my eyes blur.
I can see
An imaginary line
Connecting the horizontal tops
Of each red rock formation.

I can see the flat mesa
Of an earlier time
Stretching for miles in all directions,
Before wind and storm
Cut down into the earth
To shape these giants.

Now they stand majestically aloof
Throughout this vast valley,
Gods themselves, or homes
Worthy of the gods.

As we follow the graveled ribbon road,
Once an ancient footpath,
Up and down through
Washes and slick-rock ridges,
We meet each red stone giant
With respect and awe.

Silhouettes give us
Images not to be forgotten:
A wagon wheel,
Crouching frog, a giant mushroom,
Totem pole, teapot, old shoe,
Rooster, eagle's nest, a throne.

All together they make up
As magic a world
As ever was Alice's wonderland.

Valley of the Gods, Utah
March 2006

Family and Friends

Blair's Challenge

The last day of my visit
He asked that I write a poem
About his breakfast view.

Looking for the poetry
I glance through the window
At a tree's shaggy bark
In shades of gray and
Tinged with dusty lichen.

These textures,
And the dappled shade,
The dusty path edged in ferns,
The Victorian trim
Of the neighboring cottage
Do not speak to me.

Yet days pass
And I am still thinking
About his breakfast view.
Perhaps it steadies him each morning,
Reassuring in its sameness.

The view may be his anchor
While he reads the paper,
The window's filtered light
Reflecting the steam
Rising from his cup.

While branches soar above,
Giving shade and shelter to his home,
The tree stands solid
As his guardian.
Without it, his mornings
Would never be the same.

                    June 2005, Chautauqua, NY
                        For Blair McMillin

Chautauqua Revisited

Before the Season:

If I don't look closely
At condos rising round the edges.
It seems unchanged,
Like Brigadoon
In a timeless setting
Of hills, fields and woods.

Chautauqua did not disappear
For a hundred years.
It is I who have reappeared
To meet old friends and
Refresh the memories
Of my childhood summer home.

It is an idyllic world of trees
And lakeside cottages,
Practice houses sheltered in the woods,
Brick walks bordered by
Freshly painted Victorian homes.
And the Hotel Atheneum
Sprawling grandly along the shore.

The Plaza:

Refectory, library,
Colonnade and Bookstore
Still guard Bestor Plaza
While gardeners replant
The flower beds
To cheer the summer visitors.

Miller Park:

Miller Park, where it all began
More than a century ago,
Is cool and green beneath
A canopy of ancient trees.
The red brick bell tower
Still rings the hours,
Reminding all of us
That time is not really standing still.

The Lake:

The lake is silver
On this cloudy day.
Already trimmed with docks and buoys
It waits for the season to begin,
As yet unruffled by
The power boats and jet skis
Of summer days.

Here I daydreamed
In my father's little boat
While his line whipped past me
And the reel's whir and whine
The only sounds for miles.

The Cottage:

We walk to my grandmother's cottage
Still painted green.
Our white wicker porch furniture beckons.
Cosily nestled among the pines and ferns
The cottage is a treasure of family memories.

The Art Center:

Up on the hill,
Where I once picked wild strawberries
And carried lunch to my grandmother
Busy with her weaving classes,
The art quadrangle is silent,
Awaiting its summer students.

Uneven brick walkways pass
Beneath the colonnades
Surrounding a lush green lawn
That emits the tangy smell
Of fresh mown summer grass.

Squat white pillars
Stand stark against
The old, brown shingles.
Musty aromas of paints, clay and sawdust
Seep out through
Warped classroom doors.

Alumni Hall:

Beyond the deep, shady porch
We step into the chill gloom
Of a grandly faded Victorian house,
Home to a venerable literary society.

Walls are hung
With fragile banners.
Materials from gold thread
To rough burlap,
Reflect the goals and dreams
Of each graduating class,
A record of Chautauqua history.

Old Friends:

Behind shades of gray, soft skin, and faded eyes
We recognize our youthful selves and embrace
As if the years had not passed by.
We share some days of love and laughter
Before I say goodbye.

They will remain as always,
Attending concerts and lectures,
Anticipating family visits,
While I return to my Southwest world,
Refreshed by contact with my childhood.

Chautauqua Lake, New York, June, 2005.

Golden Anniversary

We congratulate
A golden pair of shining stars
Whose tears and joys
For fifty years
Together have been shared.

We salute
A couple rare
Whose gifts of friendship
And talents beyond compare
Have blessed so many everywhere.

We applaud
Your special day,
A milestone but not a journey done,
And hope to have the pleasure
Of your company
For many years to come.

For Sue and Beryl, June 11, 2005

First Born ("Number One Son")

Looking out the window
On a crisp October day
Through golden leaves
To a sky of piercing blue,
I am thinking
November is nearly here,
The month we have shared
For forty years.

I think of you,
A strong, handsome
Family man,
Our friend
Since childhood.

So many years have passed
Since your arrival,
Long and skinny,
After Dad and I Lamazed
Our way through the hours
To meet you.

I recall with ease
The thrill of hugging you
Tight against my shoulder,
Absorbing your warmth but
Resisting the temptation
To let love squeeze too hard.

Even now I feel
The cling of fine hair
Against my cheek,
As I held you to the window,
Loving your baby smell,
And the soft, solid weight
Of you between my hands.

I remember
Our wonder as you filled out
Little stretch suits
In a rainbow of colors,
Until you were walking
And your hair had turned
To golden curls.

All my memories of your life
Are full of fun and sharing.
Even when we moved apart
There has been no lack
Of love and caring.

May we have many years ahead
To celebrate our birthday month,
Aware of a special bond
Of mutual feelings,
As mother, son, and friends forever.

To Andy on his 40th birthday
November 17, 2005

Idaho Christmas

Morning:

The reflected sunlight,
Sparkling like a trillion diamonds,
Pierces my eyes
As my skis glide
Between the willows,
Along the wetland path.

I hope to hear a moose,
Startle a quail.
But not even a bird call
Breaks the pure silence
On this cold clear morning

It is a world of snow and ice.
The black lace of bare trees
And the distant blur of mountain firs
Complete this winter landscape.

Noon:

The hazy golden light
Of a winter's noonday sun
Comes through the
South facing windows
Turning the cabin's walls,
And furnishings
Into a mellow warm cocoon.

The stove is cold,
But the cabin is snugly warm
From the sun's determined light
While I hold Eli close
And Sam rocks at my feet.

Afternoon:

The afternoon has turned gray
When I tuck Sam snugly to my chest
And sit back in the black rocker
John bought me forty years ago
To hold our first born son.

Now it is alive once again
As we take turns
Rocking twin grandsons,
Feeling their solid weight
Against our hearts,
And inhaling the delicious perfume
Of babyhood.

Snowflakes fall across the skylight
And tree branches gently
Tap a beat in time
With the rocker's rhythm
As they wave
Against the winter sky.

Evening:

In the warmth of candlelight
We gather for our evening meal,
Two families joined by marriage
And twin boys.
The gift of new grandchildren
Brings us close again
To share a special holiday
And celebrate the blessing
Of their arrival.

Driggs, Idaho
December 2006.

Heading Home

We are flying
One hundred souls
With one hundred reasons
For being on this plane
Heading west today.

As we bump up and down
Toward altitude
I tense with mortality
And hold your arm
To ease my fears.

Behind us lies
A week on the eastern shore.
A time of celebration,
Friendship and reunion.

Ahead lies home.
For us a land of sun and mud,
Pinon trees and chamisa shrub.
A world so different
From the verdant landscape
Of Wellesley's perfect lawns.

It was a magic time
Of renewal and love,
Embracing old friends
Whose unblemished youth
Is remembered in old faces.

Fiftieth Reunion, Wellesley College
June 2007

Jim's Poem

The river,
Gripped by winter,
A black sinuous ribbon cleaves fields of white,
A harsh, colorless version of its summer self.
Silence prevails as snow falls.
I wade.
The current surges against me.
I move, searching,
The line tightens, pulses with life attached
As the fish leaves my hand.
Colors abound like springtime.
It seems so far away.

by Jim Berkenfield
Fishing on the Madison River, Montana
January 28, 2006

Still Dusting

Twenty five years ago
In a home far away
I looked on shelves of objects
Dulled by dust
And turned away.

Instead I wrote a poem
About the memories
They evoked,
While the task of dusting
Had me provoked.

Those treasures moved
To Santa Fe
And now share space
With new ones holding
Recent memories.

Pueblo pots, carvings,
Lacquer Russian boxes,
Folk art of Mexico, Peru,
Tin, glass, wood, clay and thread,
All record the passions
Of our lives
While awaiting
A feather duster's caress.

January 2008
Sequel to "Dust" on p. 20 of my book
Driving Toward the Moon

The Trio

Barefoot,
Young and
Fair of face
Timothée holds his cello
In a close embrace.

As they charm us
With dances
To Bach's cello suites.
Kate and Julie
Embody grace.

We have been welcomed
To a pure and calming space
Where enveloped
In sweet sound and movement
We are entranced
By their dance and cello union.

As his bow draws smoothly
Across the strings
Timo's strong, long fingers
Press the notes so firmly
The air vibrates
While backs arch
Toes point
And arms entwine.

I envy this artistry.
My words cannot match
Their pace
Or form melodic ties
That float and flow
Seamlessly
Between the cello
And two women dancing.

The Bach Project, Santa Fe
August 2007

Dog Days

Rill

My brother's gift
Lanky, red-haired Rill
Was an Irish Setter
Thin and edgy.
She loved upholstery
And dragging me down
City streets and cellar stairs.

Finally Mom said "enough of that!"
And Rill moved to the country
To grow gray chasing chickens
On my cousin's farm,
While we made do with rabbits,
Easter chicks, and cats.

Coco

For his eleventh birthday
Jim got his promised pup.
He chose her from a
Wriggling mass of black lab babies.
She teethed on rocks and house plants
And squirmed her way into all our hearts.

Curled up between the boys
On winter drives
Coco slept until the last
Winding mountain road
Told her we were almost there.
She could frolic in the snow
For the entire weekend.

For six years she played
Until one New Year's weekend
She lay down at John's feet
And could not get up.
Too late the vet said
To save her from the poison.

We drove her back with us
To be near Hartsdale home
In a famous cemetery
Where pets of the stars
Were her companions.

Left behind
When we moved to Santa Fe,
Last year I brought
Her ashes here
To keep Max company
In our garden.

Max

Wandering boy
Found on a highway,
He was waiting for us
At the shelter
Where we sought comfort
From our loss of Coco.

This honey-colored mutt
Greeted John with salivating joy.
We brought him home,
Where he walked with tail
Between his legs for months
Until he was sure we loved him.

Max came with us to Santa Fe
And stayed by our sides the longest.
Here he blended with the earth
And became a patient traveler
As we began our road trips
To all corners of the West.

So happy to
Go to work with John.
And when excited he
Raced in crazed circles
Around the house.

But in old age
He was anxious if left alone
Despite all our love and caring,
Until he became
Too tired to stand,
And at fifteen
We helped him go to sleep.

Molly

A twenty four hour companion,
She was ever by his side.
Her head cocked sideways
At the sound of his voice,
Or rested on his knee
While he was working.

The pads of her dainty paws
Were rough from running
On our harsh land.
Her nails tapped the tiles
As she followed us from room to room,
Never out of sight.

She walked in beauty
Of lab and golden mix,
Quiet, gentle, polite,
She loved to run and fetch
Frisbees for hours
In stream, lake, or grass
Until we surrendered in exhaustion.

Through the night
She stretched out against the bed.
At dawn she moved to the glass door
Where, with front paws crossed,
She listened to night sounds
And growled softly
At imaginary beasts.

A distant thunder rumble
Or lightening flash
Sent her shaking to our bed.
Head beneath the pillows
She trembled from nose to tail.

Of fragile health,
She tolerated pills and prods
Her soft blond coat
Reflected light
As her deep brown eyes
Followed him with devotion.

Traveling thousands of miles
She explored with us,
Sleeping on the van's back seat
And sneaking on to motel room beds.
Then one click of our turn signal
Would rouse her to give a welcome bark
As we turned in the driveway.

For six years
She was our angel
Until without warning
Disease shut her down.

While our lives go on without her
May she still walk in beauty
Chasing Frisbees among the stars.

Beau

This big bounding boy
Is the beauty of the lot.
We found this handsome
Pure-bred Golden
At a rescue home,
Not yet two years old.

A rambunctious teenager,
He came home
And learned his lessons well.
He is a blessed combination
Of one trying hard to please
Yet unable to contain
A playful, all-loving nature.

Now three,
And still a child
Who keeps us laughing,
Beau selects a squeaky toy
From his special box
To carry proudly
When we come home
And greets us with such love
We hug him with joy.

Again, we have a mellow
Traveler who
Sleeps the drive away.
Even if it lasts all day
He seems content
To be with us.
We hope he will stay on
For all our days to come.

Special friends to remember
August, 2006

Poems for Jack Parsons' Photographs

*Santa Teresa del Nino Jesus Church, El Turquillo,
New Mexico, 1999*

Beneath a dark sky
Blue tin roof and yellow walls
Define the old church.

Taos Pueblo, New Mexico, 1996

Small window leans left
Aged door jamb leans right,
Framing boards of blue.

Lake Atitlan, Guatemala, 1993

Sitting on the pier
Content between ancient posts
She looks beyond the lake.

Nabaj, Guatemala, 1993

They melt in shadow
While mountain mist rises high
O'er the turquoise house.

VW #17 from the Volkswagen Series, 1998

The orange fish swims
Across a blue green puddle
Trapped in old car rust.

VW #2 from the Volkswagen Series, 1998

The cloudy sky spreads
Above the painted river
In a land of rust.

Chateau d'Amboise, France, 2001

A crimson drape hangs
Trim in simple elegance
Concealing the world.

Gondola, Venice, 1995

From under the bridge
A slender gondola glides
On dappled water.

Speed boat wake, Lake Powell, Arizona, 1970

The trail of water
Foaming up behind the boat
Leads to twilit shore.

Inle Lake, Burma, 2003

The lake's reflection
Offers the dreamy version
Of a tranquil eve.

*Monk's robes, Mahacandayon Monastery,
Amarapura, Burma, 2003*

Suspended colors
Superimpose a pattern
Across the windows.

Shwedagon Pagoda, Yangon, Burma, 2003

Wrapped in orange folds
Buddha dreams of perfection
Lying on his side.

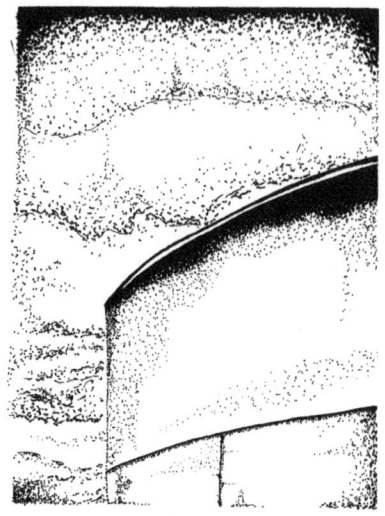

Nemrut Dagi, eastern Turkey, 2004

Sun struck sacred head,
Relic of an ancient world,
Sleeps in stony ruins.

Mosque, Ahlit, Turkey, 2004

Pleated sunlit stairs
Climb up between the shadows'
Patterns on stone walls.

Shed, County Kerry, Ireland, 2000 (two photos)

The walls of a shed
In layers of paint and rust
Create a rainbow.

Kuthodow Pagoda, Mandalay, Burma 2003

Between ghostly vaults
The massive round trees swell up
Like leafy balloons.

Sufi dancing, Istanbul, Turkey, 2004

Arms outstretched in joy
The men whirl in ecstasy
Celebrating life.

Water Tower, Santa Fe, New Mexico, 1998

Its smooth metal skin
Reflects the evening sky
At one with the clouds.

Shiprock, New Mexico, 1992

Timeless voyager
Across the Dineh domain
Secret you remain.

Poems and Susan's drawings inspired by the photos
in Jack Parsons' photo book *Ordinary Beauty*.
2007

CODA

Coda II

At the end
Of my poems
In book number one,
I placed a Coda
Just for fun.

I wrote of wondering
Who I might be,
A bird, an insect,
Mouse or bee
When I came back
In the year 5003.

Well, yesterday
I saw a wondrous bike
Of Granny Apple hue,
With no hand brakes
Or gear shifts
To make me blue.

Fifty years now
Since I last rode a bike,
So I fell in love
On very first sight.
I bought it
In a wink of eye
And rode away
In a mood so high.

If you should see me
Flying by,
Or silhouetted
Against the sky,
You will know
My life is not quite done
And I'm still out there
Having fun.

Santa Fe, May 2008

www.ingramcontent.com/pod-product-compliance
Lightning Source LLC
Chambersburg PA
CBHW021016090426
42738CB00007B/804